Vaping alters measures of vocal health

Michael M. Jones

ABSTRACT

E-cigarettes or "vapes" have become more frequently used than conventional cigarettes among youth and young adults in the U.S., however the existing research on these products and their impact on health is limited due to its modernity. The purpose of this study was to investigate the effects of various vape products on perceptual and instrumental objective measures of voice compared to a control group of nonsmokers in a sex and age-matched sample. As vapes have rapidly evolved, more substances have become available for consumers, thus a comparison was made to differentiate the effects of two common substances used in these products, specifically nicotine and cannabis. It was hypothesized that similar to a previous study, the effects of vaping on the voice may be milder as opposed to conventional cigarette smoking. The study was designed to include four groups of 10 participants each aged 18-35 including, 1) nicotine vape users, 2) cannabis vape users, 3) conventional cigarette users, and 4) a control group of nonsmokers. A total of 5 nicotine vape users, 5 cannabis vape users, one dual user of both nicotine and cannabis vapes, and 10 nonsmokers each participated in one individual data collection session to measure pulmonary function, perceptual and acoustic analysis of voice, phonatory and respiratory efficiency, and participant-rated quality of life. Cigarette smokers in this age range were unable to be recruited. Statistical analysis of the data revealed significantly higher Voice-Handicap Index-10 scores among the "all vape users" group compared to the nonsmokers, suggesting lower voice-related quality of life for vape users. No significant acoustic analysis, pulmonary function, phonatory and respiratory efficiency, or auditory-perceptual measures were identified when comparing vape users to their matched controls regardless of substance type. No significant differences were found when assessing possible differences between substance type vaped as well. It was determined that the pulmonary function measure of maximum inspiratory pressure is strongest predictor of group classification. Strong effect sizes suggest that significant measures may be seen when comparing nicotine vaping to cannabis vaping with increased sample sizes. The results of this study highlight the need for future research to continue exploring the effects of vape use along with the difference in substance type vaped on voice quality.

Table of Contents

INTRODUCTION

The History of Vaping

Electronic cigarettes ("e-cigarettes"), or "vapes," are small, handheld, battery-powered devices that heat a variety of substances (most frequently in the form of an "e-liquid") to an aerosol for users to inhale. Nicotine products are the most commonly associated substance with vapes, however, these devices are additionally capable of delivering cannabis (including THC, the primary psychoactive chemical in marijuana, as well as cannabidiol, a non-psychoactive substance derived from cannabis often referred to as "CBD"), flavorings, and other substances (Centers for Disease Control and Prevention (U.S.), 2019). Vape products are made available through a wide variety of companies with diverse branding, allowing for devices to have adopted many different shapes, sizes, types, and names since the e-cigarette was first introduced in the United States market in 2006 (Fadus et al., 2019). Given four generations of device types within the evolution of vape products presently, along with "e-cigarettes" and "vapes," these devices may be referred to in the literature and colloquially as electronic nicotine delivery systems

(ENDS), e-cigs, mods, pod-mods, vape pens, dab pens, dab rigs, and tanks (Centers for Disease

Control and Prevention, 2019). In recent years, the rise in the popularity and use of the company JUUL Labs, Inc.'s nicotine vape products has even caused the term "JUULing" to become synonymous with "vaping" among youth and young adults (Fadus et al., 2019). Given the many names these devices may go by, for the

1

purpose of this study, the term "vape" will be utilized as an umbrella term to reference all of the aforementioned products.

The exponential growth and widespread use of vapes among youth and young adults in the U.S. is a major public health concern and was declared an epidemic by the U.S. Surgeon

General in 2018 (National Center for Chronic Disease Prevention and Health Promotion (US) Office on Smoking and Health, 2016; U.S. Department of Health and Human Services, Office of

Surgeon General, 2018). Vape usage grew by 900% among high school students between 2011 to

2015, and 2.55 million U.S. middle and high school students reported vaping in 2022—including

3.3% of middle school students and 14.1% of high school students (Cooper et al., 2022; National

Center for Chronic Disease Prevention and Health Promotion (US) Office on Smoking and Health, 2016). Vape products are indeed most commonly used among young populations; however, these devices are seen across the lifespan. A Gallup poll in 2018 reported that 9% of U.S. adults regularly or occasionally vape, although the percentage of users decreases significantly as age increases (Brenan, 2018). In adults ages 18-29, 20% reported regular or occasional vaping, decreasing to 8% for ages 30-64, further diminishing to 0.5% for ages 65 and older (Newport, 2018). However, data on the specific product types or substances vaped was not collected and only the general terms of "e-cigarettes" and "vaping" were used on the surveys. In 2018, the global market for vape products was valued at about $14.05 billion, which grew to about $22.45 billion in 2022, with an expected compound annual growth rate of 30.6% from 2023 to 2030 (Bhatt et al., 2020;

Grand View Research, 2023). Among youth and young adults in the U.S., vaping has already surpassed conventional tobacco products to become the most frequently used form of tobacco (National Center for Chronic Disease Prevention and Health Promotion (US) Office on Smoking and Health, 2016). As these growing statistics suggest, this trend will likely continue while the technology rapidly advances to even more convenient forms. It is plausible that continued vaping throughout the lifespan may eventually lead to a significant increase in the percentage of older adults who use these products.

The Effect of Vaping on Health

The advent of the vape signified the shift from conventional cigarette smoking to its hightech successor in the extensive lineage and history of tobacco products in the United States. Initially acclaimed as a smoking cessation tool when first introduced in the U.S., these devices were also publicized as a safer alternative to cigarette smoking (Fadus et al., 2019). They were thought by many to be less harmful than traditional cigarette smoking, considering no combustion takes place during the heating process and the aerosolized e-liquids are free of tobacco tar (Biondi-Zoccai et al., 2019). Bernat et al. (2018) examined the perceptions of the benefits and risks of nicotine vape product usage among Florida adolescents and reported that less than one-half of their participants indicated that vaping is harmful to their health, with 43% of youth stating that vapes are less harmful than conventional cigarettes. Surprisingly, and contrary to many vaping prevention advertisements for youths, less than 15% of the sample cited a benefit of vaping as

a means to "look cool" and "have more friends;" rather, between onequarter and one-third of the sample suggested that the benefits of vaping include stress relief and a sense of comfort at social events (Bernat et al., 2018). This study does note that current vape use correlated with increased odds of a participant reporting that vapes are less harmful than cigarettes, along with decreased odds of reporting that vapes are harmful to one's health when compared to youth committed to never using vape products. These attitudes towards vaping were confirmed by Romijnders et al. (2018) in their narrative literature review that assessed 65 studies published between 2010 and 2018, reporting the perceptions of both adults and youth regarding vape use. Overall, nicotine vape products were perceived by both adult and youth users to be not only healthier and safer than traditional cigarette smoking, but also less addictive, safer for one's social environment, and even safer to use during pregnancy (Romijnders et al., 2018). However,
this narrative literature review does indicate that trends in the more recent literature suggest that the risk perception of vaping may be on the rise among both adults and youth.

These popular beliefs and perceptions of vaping are not based on evidence, and since these devices are relatively new and continue to evolve, the research is limited concerning the effects they might have on the human body. Contrary to the idea that vaping is less addictive, studies have shown that some of these devices are capable of delivering concentrations of nicotine comparable to or exceeding that of conventional cigarettes, placing users at an equal or higher risk of nicotine addiction (Dinardo & Rome, 2019; Fadus et al., 2019). For example, the popular pod-mod

JUUL devices contain 0.7 mL of e-liquid per pod, which in full delivers the nicotine content equal to about 20 cigarettes (Dinardo & Rome, 2019; Shao & Friedman, 2020). Leavens et al. (2019) indicate that of their 979 U.S. adult participants, daily JUUL users reported using approximately 10 pods per month, with the overall sample averaging 4 pods per month. Furthermore, Wagoner et al. (2021) detail that of their young adult sample who reported JUUL use at least every couple of months, 21.6% stated that one JUUL pod lasts one day or less. In addition, the current literature does not support the claim that vapes may be utilized as a tool for smoking cessation, its purported original intention, rather, vaping may be correlated with an elevated risk of user experimentation with conventional tobacco products as well as traditional drugs of abuse (Eltorai et al., 2019). Nicotine is an addictive substance with known adverse effects on the human body, especially with regard to the developing adolescent brain, including impacts on learning, memory, and attention (U.S. Department of Health and Human Services, Office of Surgeon General, 2018). However, nicotine is not the only substance comprising the ingredients list of the nicotine-based e-liquids. A growing body of evidence has shown there to be a number of toxic organic and inorganic chemicals found in both the e-liquids and aerosols (Zhao et al., 2020). Dinardo & Rome (2019) summarize chemicals found in vape products, some of which are known irritants of the respiratory mucosa and carcinogens, such as acetaldehyde and formaldehyde, particulate matter, and various metals (including chromium, cadmium, nickel, and lead). Heavy metals present in the vaping aerosols are suspected to originate from the metal coils built into the devices that are used to heat the e-liquids, and their inhalation may result in serious health effects such as cancer, cardiovascular disease, renal damage, and neurotoxicity (Zhao et al., 2020). In fact, there is no research in the scientific literature indicating the existence of vape products that do not contain harmful chemicals. The chemicals commonly found in these products are associated with severe health conditions, thus establishing the critical necessity for thorough analyses on their impact.

The long-term implications of vaping on human physiology are largely undetermined given their modernity, however, the long-term effects shown in studies with animal subjects alongside the acute effects in human subjects indicate the need for caution and further research (Tsai et al., 2020). In their review, Tsai et al. (2020) analyzed a total of 40 studies investigating the cardiopulmonary physiological changes caused by vape use on either animal or human subjects. Their review found that acute exposure to vaping aerosols increased blood pressure and heart rate in human subjects, and chronic exposure with animal subjects led to increased arterial stiffness, vascular endothelial changes, increased angiogenesis, cardiorenal fibrosis, and increased formation of atherosclerotic plaques (Tsai et al., 2020). Likewise, the acute pulmonary effects in human subjects include increased airway flow resistance and increased airway reactivity, with the long-term effects in animal subjects including emphysema, higher airway resistance, airway obstruction, and airway inflammation (Tsai et al., 2020). The reviewed studies provide evidence that inhalation of vaping aerosols for even 5 minutes has the potential to impact airway flow resistance, and inhalation for 30 minutes was shown to decrease vital capacity (Antoniewicz et al., 2019; Tsai et al., 2020). Along with these physiological effects, research is beginning to reveal the correlation of vaping with greater mental health concerns, including reports of increased rates of anxiety, ADHD, PTSD, low self-esteem, gambling disorder, and impulsivity among young adult vape users (Becker et al., 2021; Grant et al., 2019). The health implications continue to accumulate and yet there is still much to investigate with further studies needed to fully understand the lasting impacts in the areas that researchers have already examined.

The Effects of Traditional Smoking on Vocal Function

While numerous studies have assessed the impact of vaping on cardiac and pulmonary physiology, mental health, as well as the chemicals found in the aerosols themselves, there is a paucity of evidence with regard to how vape use might impact the voice. As the newest innovation in smoking, it is necessary to consider that vaping might impact vocal function in a similar way as compared to its predecessor of conventional cigarette smoking or even traditional combustible marijuana, considering vapes are capable of delivering cannabis as well. Traditional forms of smoking have been shown to have a number of adverse effects on the components of voice production. A meta-analysis conducted by Byeon & Cha (2020) reports that the most significant impact of smoking on the voice is the lowering of fundamental frequency (F_0), or the acoustic correlate of what we perceive as pitch in the voice defined as the number of vibratory cycles of the vocal folds per second, as well as the reduction of maximum phonation time (MPT), a measure of phonatory and respiratory efficiency defined as the longest duration in which an individual can sustain consistent vowel production. Smoking has been shown to irritate the vocal folds, dry vocal fold mucosa, and can lead to inflammation and organic voice disorders such as laryngeal cancer (Byeon & Cha, 2020; Tuhanioğlu et al., 2019). One reviewed study contended that increased mass of the vocal folds due to inflammation and edema causes a decrease in their rate of vibration, leading to the observed reduction in F_0 (Byeon & Cha, 2020;

Pinar et al., 2016). Ayoub et al. (2019) showed that these effects of smoking on laryngeal function are consistent across languages and their differences in the nature of vowel production, accounting for both lower F_0 and speaking fundamental frequency (SFF), or the average F_0 in connected speech, in cigarette smokers. The weakening of pulmonary function is likewise associated with smoking, elucidating the reductions seen during MPT trials (Byeon & Cha, 2020). As noted earlier, studies have already begun to show the impact of vaping on pulmonary function, suggesting that vaping may similarly reduce MPT. It is possible, then, that deviant values in the s/z ratio—another measure of phonatory and respiratory efficiency— may also be seen as a result of vaping. As another task that relies on sustained sound production, the s/z ratio compares the longest duration for the voiceless/voiced consonant pairs of /s/ and /z/. An s/z ratio divergent from 1.0 along with shortened durations of either phoneme may be possible indicators of respiratory and/or laryngeal dysfunction (Kent et al., 1987). Consistent with these findings on the objective, instrumental measures of voice, smokers have self-reported higher (worse) scores than nonsmokers on the Voice Handicap Index (VHI), a subjective evaluation of an individual's own voice where higher scores imply vocal dissatisfaction in everyday life (Ayoub et al., 2019). Although not as prevalent in the literature due to its only recent widespread legalization throughout parts of the United States, marijuana smoking may also impact vocal function. In their systematic review, Meehan-Atrash et al. (2019) report that about half of the U.S. population has tried cannabis, nonetheless, its impact on voice production appears to be similar to that of tobacco smoking. Complaints of hoarseness, breathiness, and weakness were the most common findings in marijuana smokers as indicated by Balouch et al. (2022). Most studies on marijuana smoking likewise reveal increased airflow resistance, airway inflammation, respiratory distress, congestion, cough, and darkened vocal folds in a dose-response relationship (Meehan-Atrash et al., 2019). In addition, an increased risk of laryngeal cancer was also determined to be directly associated with cannabis smoking (Valentino & McKinnon, 2019). Given these adverse effects of traditional marijuana smoking on the voice, Meehan-Atrash et al. (2019) recognize the fact that vapes capable of delivering cannabis have not yet been thoroughly investigated for safety.

The Effects of Vaping on Vocal Function

Few studies have directly investigated the effect of vaping on vocal function. Tuhanioğlu et al. (2019) completed a cross-sectional study comprised of 81 healthy adult men separated into three groups: nicotine vape users, conventional cigarette users, and nonsmokers who had reported never smoking. Both subjective and objective measures of voice were compared across groups, including the subjective measure of the Voice Handicap Index 10 (VHI-10), along with the following objective measures: F_0, perturbation measures of jitter %, shimmer %, and shimmer dB (jitter and shimmer signify variations in frequency and amplitude of the voice and are correlated with deviant voice characteristics such as hoarseness and roughness), and harmonics-to-noise ratio (HNR) values (a means of quantifying the degree of additive noise in voice production) (Ferrand, 2002; Tuhanioğlu et al., 2019). Overall, they found significantly lower VHI-10 scores reported in the vape users compared to that of the cigarette smoking users, suggesting that individual perceptions of quality of voice were better in the vape user group (Tuhanioğlu et al., 2019). The only other significant differences reported between groups were that of higher (worse) shimmer dB and lower (worse) HNR in the cigarette smoking group compared to both the vape user and control group. In addition, F_0 was higher in the vaping group compared to cigarette smokers, although this result was not significant (Tuhanioğlu et al., 2019). The study concluded that the effect of vaping on voice quality might be considered as mild compared to that of conventional cigarette smoking, positing that this may be due to lower toxin content and higher vapor content present in vape products compared to conventional cigarettes (Tuhanioğlu et al., 2019).

A similar study conducted by Dingmann (2021) compared objective vocal measures of 18 individuals to the user's own rating of their vocal quality across the same three groups as Tuhanioğlu et al. (2019): nicotine vape users, conventional cigarette users, and nonsmokers that had reported never smoking. Similarly, no significant differences across all objective vocal measures were reported, including jitter %, shimmer %, F_0, intensity, and HNR. Subjects in this study also participated in two self-perception measures, the Voice Handicap Index (VHI) and a survey taken from the study conducted by Bernat et al. (2018) to assess the risk perceptions of smoking and vaping. Surprisingly, while the average scores on the VHI varied among the three groups, each average fell within normal limits with no significant differences (Dingmann, 2021). On the risk perception survey, both nonuser and vape users overwhelmingly identified vaping as less or equally harmful than tobacco cigarettes, contrasting with conventional cigarette users who reported the exact opposite (Dingmann, 2021).

Dealino & Dela Cruz (2022) used the Filipino translation of the original 30-item Voice Handicap Index (Umali & Hernandez, 2006, as cited by Lim, Hernandez and Gonzalo, 2010) to compare a sample of 26 conventional cigarette smokers and 26 nicotine vape users in the age range of 18-65. Unlike Tuhanioğlu et al. (2019), no statistically significant difference was found when contrasting Filipino VHI scores of the conventional smokers and nicotine vape users (Dealino & Dela Cruz, 2022). However, it is important to note the plausibility that differences observed across the three studies of Tuhanioğlu et al. (2019), Dingmann (2021), and Dealino & Dela Cruz (2022) may be due to cultural differences in perceptions of voice quality as the three studies were conducted in Turkey, the Philippines, and the United States, respectively. Yiu et al. (2008) and Yiu et al. (2011) report the necessity to consider cultural and language backgrounds of raters in a clinical voice evaluation, as different backgrounds can impact the perception of voice disorders.

Likewise, differences may have been observed due to use of the 10 question VHI-10 versus the 30 question VHI across the three studies.

A study completed by Sample (2019) utilized videostroboscopic analysis of the vocal folds in 7 vape users, 4 cigarette smokers, and 6 non-smokers in addition to the acoustic analysis. The results indicated a significant relationship between vape use and abnormal vocal fold parameters viewed with stroboscopy, including abnormal mucosal wave, free edge contour, phase closure, vocal fold varices, and vocal fold edema (Sample, 2019). This study likewise reported no significant relationship with vape use and abnormal acoustic measures of F_0 and the perturbation measures of jitter and shimmer.

Two studies investigated the impact of e-cigarette vapor extract (ECVE) on vocal fold mucosa using an in vitro study design. Lungova et al. (2022) exposed human engineered vocal fold mucosa to different concentrations of ECVE for 1 week, resulting in damage to luminal cells, disruption of homeostasis and innate immune responses, and intense epithelial remodeling. Martinez et al. (2023) similarly exposed cultured vocal fold fibroblasts (hVFFs) to ECVE with and without nicotine and compared the results to hVFFs exposed to cigarette smoke extract (CSE). They concluded that ECVE induced cytotoxicity in hVFFs, but CSE caused greater cellular responses such as evidence of DNA damage, suggesting that conventional cigarettes may be more harmful than e-cigarettes to laryngeal tissues in a shorter time frame (Martinez et al., 2023). Both studies support the notion that e-cigarette vapor may negatively impact the vocal fold mucosa, which in turn may cause adverse acoustic changes to the voice.

Despite these preliminary findings, all of the above-mentioned studies

highlight the need for further research on the impact of vape use on vocal function.

While there are few limitations to the Tuhanioğlu et al. (2019) study, the

participants in this study included only men of ages 18 to 54 years. The inclusion of

only male participants may control for the anatomical differences in the larynx

based on sex that may lead to differing acoustic results, but this is not representative

of the population as a whole, as people of both sexes use these products. Further

research that includes groups of both sexes that are age-matched may increase the

validity of the results. Dingmann (2021) did include both male and female subjects

in their study; however, there was not an equivalent distribution of gender among

the groups (assuming "gender" in this study refers to biological sex), suggesting

that the differences noted might have been attributable in part to differences in sex

in addition to smoking habits. Both Dingmann (2021), Sample (2019), and Dealino

& Dela Cruz (2022) discuss limitations due to a small number of participants,

resulting perhaps in patterns that may not be representative of the population as a

whole. Increasing the sample size in further studies with a sufficient number of

participants to ensure the use of parametric statistics may likewise increase the

validity of the results. Dealino & Dela Cruz

(2022) also state that further studies would benefit from inclusion of a control group

of nonsmokers when investigating this population using the VHI. Lastly, Dingmann

(2021) clarifies that the quality of participant voice recordings in their study could

not be controlled due to the use of participants' personal computers and built-in

microphones in the context of an online Zoom meeting. Differing equipment, distance from the microphone, and various background noise may have led to inaccurate measurements. Research utilizing a controlled data collection environment is necessary to avoid threats to validity. The limitations of these three studies indicate the need for additional examination of this topic.

Purpose of the Study

The purpose of the present study was to investigate and add to the literature the effects of various vape products on perceptual and instrumental objective measures of voice in a sex and age-matched sample. Previous studies have solely focused on nicotine vapes in comparison to conventional cigarette smoking. The current study aimed to contrast both nicotine and cannabis vape products to conventional cigarette smoking and a control group of nonsmokers. In addition, measures of inspiratory and expiratory pressure were collected in order to characterize pulmonary function. It was hypothesized, similar to Tuhanioğlu et al. (2019), that the effects of vape products on the voice may be milder as opposed to conventional cigarette smoking; however, provided the evidence of weakened pulmonary function with vaping, reductions in measures of phonatory and respiratory efficiency may be observed. The differences between substances inhaled (nicotine-based products versus cannabis) is unknown. Therefore, this study was designed to answer the following research questions:

Research Question 1: Do the perceptual and instrumental objective measures of voice and respiratory pressure differ among vape users, conventional cigarette smokers, and non-users?

Research Question 1a: Does the substance type (nicotine vs cannabis) inhaled via a vape impact the perceptual and instrumental objective measures of vocal function and respiratory pressure?

Research Question 1b: Does the delivery method for nicotine products (nicotine vapes vs conventional cigarettes) impact the perceptual and instrumental objective measures of vocal function and respiratory pressure?

Research Question 2: Are there patterns of perceptual, objective, and quality of life measures that distinguish among the subject groups?

Research Question 2a: What are the correlational relationships among the clinician-rated perceptual measures, the instrumental objective measures, and the subject-rated quality of life measures of vocal function?

Research Question 2b: What combinations of these measures tend to discriminate between delivery method groups (nicotine vapes vs conventional cigarettes)?

Research Question 2c: What combinations of these measures tend to discriminate between substance type (nicotine vs cannabis) inhaled via a vape?

The results of this study will add to the literature on the possible adverse health implications that may be associated with vape use, particularly within the area of vocal health and hygiene. The evidence provided by this study may allow health professionals to appropriately guide and inform individuals they serve on the effects of vaping, thus allowing users to make an informed decision regarding smoking habits.

METHODOLOGY

This is a descriptive comparative study with a between-subjects design and was planned to include a total of four groups: nicotine vape users, cannabis vape users, cigarette smokers, and a control group of nonsmokers who have never smoked. Individuals were measured at one time point at the UW-Milwaukee Swallow Physiology Laboratory during a 45-minute session. The outcome measures for the current study were divided into five categories: 1) the acoustic analysis measures of fundamental frequency (F_0), jitter %, shimmer %, shimmer dB, harmonics-to-noise ratio (HNR), and mean intensity dB; 2) the pulmonary function measures of maximum inspiratory pressure (MIP) and maximum expiratory pressure (MEP); 3) the phonatory and respiratory efficiency measures of maximum phonation time (MPT) and s/z ratio; 4) the auditory-perceptual measure of the Consensus Auditory-Perceptual Evaluation of Voice (CAPE-
V) ratings; and 5) the quality of life measure of the Voice Handicap Index-10 (VHI-
10) scores.

Subjects and Recruitment

This study was planned to enroll 40 healthy individuals between ages 18 and 35. This age range was selected to reflect the higher percentage of vape use seen in the young adult population (20% of adults ages 18-29 report regular or occasional vaping in 2018, decreasing to 8% for ages 30-64) (Newport, 2018). Subjects were recruited from South-East Wisconsin and Northern Illinois. Multiple methods of recruitment were utilized, including posting approved flyers on university campuses, sending emails with research recruitment information to university staff, social media posts, and word of mouth. Participants were also recruited through personal contact. Eligible participants were between ages 18 and 35 that belong to one of the following groups: nicotine vape users, cannabis vape users, cigarette smokers, and nonsmokers.

Nicotine vape users were defined as individuals who have used a nicotine vape daily for at least one year with no cigarette use for at least one year prior to data collection. Cannabis vape users were defined as individuals who have used a cannabis vape daily for at least one year with no cigarette or nicotine vape use for at least one year prior to data collection. Cigarette smokers were defined as individuals who smoke at least two cigarettes per day for at least one year with no vape use for at least one year prior to data collection. Nonsmokers were defined as individuals with no history of vape or cigarette use.

Participants in the vape and smoking groups were sex and age-matched within 3 years to a non-smoking control subject. Age was a factor in order to account for possible continued development of the larynx for younger subjects and possible structural changes of the larynx due to aging that may become apparent as early as the third or fourth decade of life that may impact acoustic and perceptual measurements (Ferrand, 2019). Although typically older adults are matched within 5 years (Orlikoff et al, 2022), the range of 3 years was selected for this study given the likelihood of young adult participants as this is the population that generally

uses vape products compared to likely accruals of older cigarette smoking

participants. Biological sex was a factor in this study in order to account for the

anatomical differences in the larynx observed between male and female participants

that lead to distinctions in acoustic and perceptual measurements. Therefore, an

equivalent distribution of biological sex across groups was required. Race was not a

factor in this study.

Individuals that were excluded from the study included persons with any

current diagnosis of a vocal fold pathology or currently receiving voice therapy

services, gastroesophageal reflux disease (GERD), current respiratory/sinus

infections, or any other health condition that may adversely affect respiratory or

laryngeal health. Likewise, individuals with a history of chronic overuse/abuse of

the voice were excluded from the study. All participants were provided with an

explanation of the study procedures and had an opportunity to ask questions of the

researcher. Participants then provided written consent prior to engaging in the study

procedures. Monetary compensation was provided to participants following the

completion of procedures.

Materials

Acoustic analysis was completed based on the sustained /a/ task and using the

Boersma & Weenink (2023) voice analysis computer program, *Praat.* This software

is currently one of the leading voice analysis programs and provided the following

quantitative data for this study:

fundamental frequency (F_0), jitter %, shimmer %, shimmer dB, harmonics-to-noise ratio (HNR), and mean intensity dB, in order to match the objective data collected by Tuhanioğlu et al. (2019). These acoustic parameters are validated, objective measures of voice that are widely used as diagnostic indicators of vocal pathology, forms of biofeedback, markers for progress in voice therapy, and baseline and outcome measures in research (Ferrand, 2019; Lourenço et al., 2014). Lourenço et al. (2014) report that abnormal F_0, high jitter and shimmer, and low HNR and intensity are all potential reflections of dysphonia or dysfunction related to vocal pathology.

Voice samples were recorded in a sound-treated booth with the digital audio recording software

Audacity using a Blue Yeti USB condenser microphone connected to a MacBook Pro (13-inch, 2020, Four Thunderbolt 3 ports). A subject mouth-to-microphone distance of 6 inches was maintained during the recording. Acoustic analysis was completed with the *Praat* software. Voice samples were stored using a secure Microsoft OneDrive cloud storage system in order to protect participant confidentiality.

Measures of pulmonary function were conducted with the MicroRPM Respiratory Pressure Meter (Figure 1). This device provided objective measures of maximum inspiratory pressure (MIP) and maximum expiratory pressure (MEP). These parameters reflect the relative strength of the respiratory muscles, with deviant pressure values indicating possible pulmonary weakness and pathology (Choi et al., 2017).

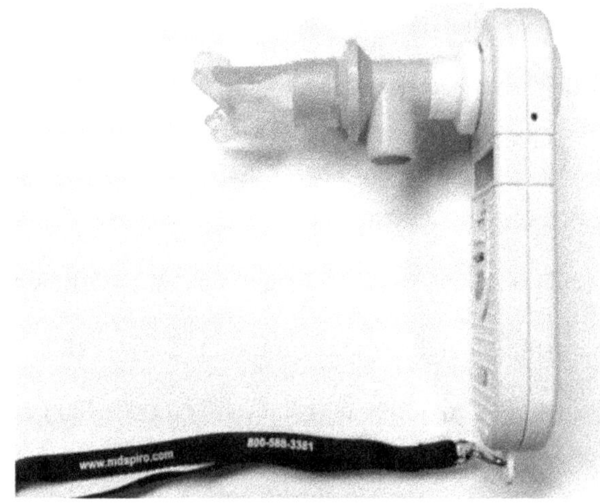

The Consensus Auditory-Perceptual Evaluation of Voice (CAPE-V) (Figure 2) was administered as a subjective, clinician-rated assessment of the auditory-perceptual qualities of voice. Clinicians rate roughness (defined as perceived irregularity in the voice), breathiness (defined as audible air escape in the voice), strain (defined as perceived excessive vocal effort or hyperfunction), pitch, loudness, and overall severity of the voice through a series of standardized tasks developed by Kempster et al. (2009). Tasks include 1) sustained vowels, 2) reading six specific sentences with differing phonetic contexts, and 3) natural running speech in response to the prompt, "tell me about your voice problem" or "tell me how your voice is functioning." While the CAPE-V protocol calls for the standard interview questions listed above, the prompts were adjusted to "tell me about your job, favorite vacation, or weekend plans" in order to elicit a longer and more natural sounding speech sample.

A visual analog scale (VAS) is used to assess each attribute. While listening

to an individual's voice, the listener creates a tick mark on a 100-mm line for each

quality, with a value of 0 representing an absence of deviance in a specific quality

and 100 representing a severely deviant quality. Each quality is prescribed with a

"C" for a consistent quality or "I" for an intermittent quality. The CAPE-V form

also allows for comments on resonance and other additional features of the voice

such as aphonia, tremor, vocal fry, and diplophonia.

Figure 2. Consensus Auditory-Perceptual Evaluation of Voice (CAPE-V)
Protocol (Kempster et al., 2009)

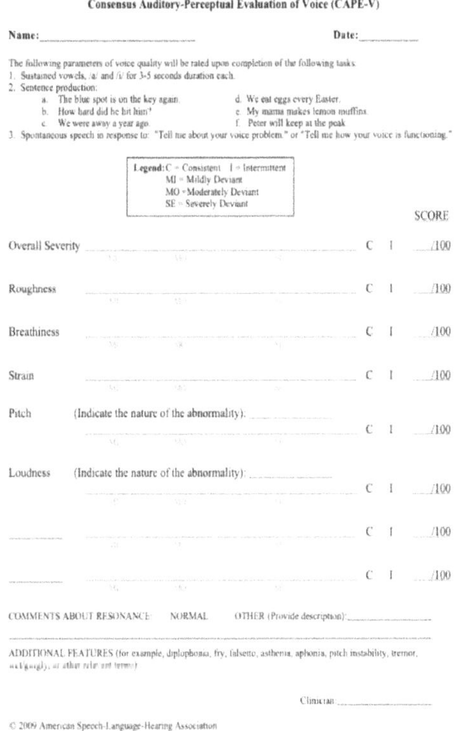

All participants completed the Voice Handicap Index-10 (VHI-10) (Figure

3), a subjective, self-rated survey rating quality of life in relation to experiences with vocal quality (Rosen et al., 2004). This short survey consists of 10 questions to assess an individual's selfperception of their voice and the circumstances associated with their possible voice issues. Ratings are made on a 5-point ordinal scale. Increasing scores correlate with increasing negative quality of life due to voice concerns; scores above 11 are considered abnormal and may be associated with vocal pathology (Arffa et al., 2012).

Figure 3. Voice Handicap Index-10 (Rosen et al., 2004)

Voice Handicap Index (VHI)-10

Instructions: These are statements that many people have used to describe their voices and the effects of their voices on their lives. Circle the response that indicates how frequently you have the same experience.

0-Never	1-Almost Never	2-Sometimes	3-Almost Always	4-Always

	0	1	2	3	4
My voice makes it difficult for people to hear me.	0	1	2	3	4
People have difficulty understanding me in a noisy room.	0	1	2	3	4
My voice difficulties restrict personal and social life.	0	1	2	3	4
I feel left out of conversations because of my voice.	0	1	2	3	4
My voice problem causes me to lose income.	0	1	2	3	4
I feel as though I have to strain to produce voice.	0	1	2	3	4
The clarity of my voice is unpredictable.	0	1	2	3	4
My voice problem upsets me.	0	1	2	3	4
My voice makes me feel handicapped.	0	1	2	3	4
People ask, "What's wrong with your voice?"	0	1	2	3	4

Procedures

All participants attended a single 45-minute data-collection session at the UW-Milwaukee Swallow Physiology Laboratory. All vape users were asked to refrain from vaping for at least 30 minutes before their session as a means to reduce the variability of each individual's time since they last used their product. Subjects were asked about the last time they used their product in order to assess the possible impact of this extraneous variable. The following procedures were then completed in the same order for each participant following a set of uniform instructions from the researcher. All instruments were calibrated per manual instructions and manufacturer recommendations prior to data collection.

Subject-Reported Measures (Quality of Life)

The 45-minute data collection sessions started with the self-rated quality of life measure of the VHI-10 completed by each participant via a Qualtrics survey interface in the UWM Swallow Physiology Laboratory. The self-rated measure was completed prior to voice production tasks to avoid unintentional alterations in perceptions of voice that participants may have experienced based on their performance during the tasks.

Pulmonary Function Measures

Objective measures began with the assessment of pulmonary function through the use of a MicroRPM Respiratory Pressure Meter. Subjects were instructed following the MicroRPM operating manual procedures for maximum inspiratory pressure (MIP) and maximum expiratory pressure (MEP). For MIP, participants completed a maximum exhalation and then executed a forced maximal inhalation against the device for as long as possible (with a minimum of 2 seconds) while in a seated position (Micro Direct, Inc., 2019). The researcher demonstrated the task to ensure participant understanding. Participants repeated this test three times, and the highest pressure was used as the MIP. For MEP, subjects completed a maximum inhalation and then executed a forced exhalation against the device for as long as possible (with a minimum of 2 seconds) while in a seated position (Micro Direct, Inc., 2019). The researcher demonstrated the task as well to ensure understanding. Participants repeated this test three times and the highest pressure was used as the MEP. A one-minute rest period between trials was offered to avoid participant fatigue or presyncope (light-headedness).

Auditory-Perceptual and Acoustic Analysis

The auditory-perceptual assessment CAPE-V was then administered, which included simultaneous audio recordings of voice samples that were used for later acoustic analysis. Participants were seated in a sound-treated booth with a microphone positioned six inches from their mouth. The researcher instructed each participant through the speech tasks of the CAPE-V protocol (Figure 2), with one modification. In order to parallel the procedures of Tuhanioğlu et al. (2019), the first CAPE-V speech task of sustaining /a/ for 3-5 seconds was completed three times instead of once. Subjects were instructed to produce the sustained /a/ at a comfortable pitch and loudness. A 1-second middle segment for each trial was then selected in order to avoid variability of voicing due to onset and offset (Tuhanioğlu et al., 2019). Each 1-second segment was analyzed later for all acoustic parameters using the *Praat* software. The remainder of the CAPE-V was then administered, with continued recording of all speech tasks. The researcher completed CAPE-V ratings simultaneously as subjects perform the speech tasks. Deidentified recordings of the completed CAPE-V tasks for each participant were rated again at a later time by two trained graduate student listeners blind to subject group in order to assess interjudge reliability. The student researcher also re-rated the samples from the voice recordings in a blinded manner selected by the research mentor as a measure of intrajudge reliability. Intraclass correlations for interjudge reliability ranged from 0.66 for strain to 1.0 for pitch and loudness, and intrajudge reliability ranged from 0.73 for strain to 1.0 for pitch. These reliability values are consistent with those reported by Zraick et al. (2011) in their study establishing the validity of the CAPE-V.

Phonatory and Respiratory Efficiency Measures

The data collection session ended with measures of phonatory and respiratory efficiency. For the maximum phonation task, subjects were instructed to take a deep breath and sustain /a/ on one exhalation for as long as they could at a comfortable pitch and loudness. In order to ensure participant understanding, the researcher demonstrated an abbreviated version of the task. This task was completed and recorded three times, with an offered one-minute rest period between trials. The longest duration was used as the MPT. Reduced duration of MPT may be an indication of possible respiratory deficiency or vocal dysfunction and laryngeal

pathology (Kent et al., 1987).

Finally, subjects completed the s/z ratio task. Participants were instructed to

take a deep breath and sustain /s/ on one exhale for as long as they could. The

researcher demonstrated an abbreviated version of the task. Subjects completed the

/s/ task twice, and then repeated the task by sustaining /z/ for as long as possible for

two trials. The longer recorded duration for each phoneme was used to calculate the

ratio of /s/ to /z/. The s/z ratio values divergent from 1.0 along with shortened

durations of either phoneme may be possible indicators of respiratory and/or

laryngeal dysfunction (Kent et al., 1987).

Both phonatory and respiratory efficiency measures were calculated using the

Praat software. All data were stored using a secure Microsoft OneDrive cloud

storage system.

Statistical Analysis Plan

Statistical analysis was conducted with SPSS v.28 (IBM, 2021).

Descriptive statistics for all outcome measures were determined. Means and

standard deviations were calculated for the acoustic analysis measures (F_0, jitter %,

shimmer %, shimmer dB, HNR, and mean intensity dB), pulmonary function

measures (MIP and MEP), phonatory and respiratory efficiency measures (MPT

and s/z ratio), and the visual analog scale ratings of the CAPE-V. Medians and

semiinterquartile range were used to characterize quality of life ratings on the VHI-

10.

Inferential statistics were used to determine whether there were significant differences among the dependent variables as a function of subject group. For Research Question 1, all acoustic analysis measures (F_0, jitter %, shimmer %, shimmer dB, HNR, and mean intensity dB), pulmonary function measures (MIP and MEP), phonatory and respiratory efficiency measures (MPT and s/z ratio), and the visual analog scale ratings of the CAPE-V were tested for normality and sphericity. If all assumptions for parametric statistics were met, then the appropriate parametric analysis of variance (One-Way ANOVA for independent groups and repeated measures ANOVA for related groups) were planned for use with these measures, followed up with appropriate two-group comparisons (independent or paired t-test) to assess significant differences between pairs of groups. If assumptions for parametric statistics were not met, the non-parametric equivalents were planned (i.e., the Kruskal-Wallis One-Way ANOVA followed by the Mann-Whitney U test for independent groups or the Friedman Two-Way ANOVA followed by the Wilcoxon Signed Rank test for related groups).

Because VHI-10 data are ordinal, they were planned to be assessed for significant differences among groups using the Kruskal-Wallis One-Way ANOVA followed by the MannWhitney U test for independent groups and the Friedman Two-Way ANOVA followed by the Wilcoxon Signed Rank test for related groups.

Bonferroni adjustment was planned for all post-hoc testing in order to control experiment-wide error rate.

For Research Question 2, bivariate correlations were first calculated among all 18 dependent variables to determine the degree of intercorrelation among measures. These were used to reduce redundancy and assist in the selection of predictors for further regression analysis. The appropriate statistic, either Pearson's r or Spearman's rho, was used depending upon the level of measurement of the dependent measures being correlated.

Once a set of predictor measures was selected, logistic regression was used to determine the relationship between the predictors and their ability to categorize participants into appropriate user groups.

RESULTS

The purpose of the present study was to investigate the possible impact of various vape products on perceptual and instrumental objective measures of voice in a sex and age-matched sample. As no studies to date have compared differences in substances being vaped in this context, it was planned to contrast the effects of nicotine and cannabis vape products to conventional cigarette smoking and a control group of nonsmokers.

Participants

Twenty-one (21) healthy adults met the eligibility criteria to participate in the study. The nicotine vape user group consisted of 3 males and 2 females, aged between 20-30 years (mean = 25.40 years; SD = 4.16). The cannabis vape user group consisted of 3 males and 2 females, aged between 22-30 years, (mean = 25.8

years; SD = 3.03). When combining the nicotine vape and cannabis vape users along with one additional participant into an "all vape users" group, this group consisted of 6 males and 5 females, aged between 20-30 years (mean = 25.45; SD = 3.30).

The nonsmoker control group consisted of 5 males and 5 females, aged between 18-30 years (mean = 24.20 years, SD = 3.43).

Each vape user participant was sex and age-matched within 3 years to a non-smoking control subject. Due to uneven recruitment of control subjects and vape user subjects, one male control subject was matched to one participant in both the nicotine and cannabis vape groups, resulting in sample sizes N = 11 for the "all vapers users" group and N = 10 for the non-smoking control group. Cigarette smokers that met eligibility criteria were unable to be recruited for this study.

Pearson's Chi-Squared test (X^2) was performed on the variable of sex across all three groups, yielding no significant differences among groups based on sex (X^2 = 0.202, df = 2, p = 0.904). To determine differences of the variable of age across groups, the Kruskal-Wallis Test was used. Similarly, no significant differences among all three groups were observed based on age (p = 0.662). Therefore, the vape user groups and control groups were equivalent based on subject demographics.

Eligibility criteria for the vape groups initially required at least one year of daily use of their respective products without other product use. As reports of dual use became common during recruitment, this factor proved to be a significant barrier to accruals if eligibility criteria remained so restrictive. Thus, subjects were instead divided into groups based on the product they described as using daily for at least one year. Subjects that indicated daily use of one product along with "occasional" or "social" use of another product were assigned to the group based on the daily product used. "Occasional" or "social" use was subjectively defined by participants using descriptions such as "once per week" or "just on the weekends if offered by a friend." Given this adjustment to definition of user groups, two of the five nicotine vape users reported occasional cannabis use, one of which occasionally used both combustible and vape delivery methods. One of the five cannabis vape users reported social use of a nicotine vape, and three of the five described occasional combustible cannabis use. One participant in this study reported daily use of both nicotine and cannabis vapes with "social" use of combustible cannabis, and this individual was placed solely in the "all vape users" group.

The nicotine vape group's duration of use ranged from 2 to 6.5 years (mean = 5.3 years, SD = 1.86) with subject-reported approximate puffs per day ranging from 15 to 150 (mean = 68 puffs per day, SD = 56.41). The cannabis vape group's duration of use ranged from 1 to 17 years (mean = 5.1 years, SD = 6.69) with approximate puffs per day ranging from 2 to 45 (mean = 13.5 puffs per day, SD = 17.94). When combining the two vape groups into the "all vape users" group, duration of use ranged from 1 to 17 years (mean = 5.27 years, SD = 4.40) with approximate puffs per day ranging from 2 to 150 (mean = 37.45 puffs per day, SD = 47.58).   Prior to collection of outcome measures, participants were asked to briefly describe the type of product that they use and the approximate duration since the last time they used it. Nicotine vape users reported using primarily disposable products with no temperature setting options. Nicotine vape product brands included JUUL, Posh, Vuse, Breeze, and Elf Bar. Duration since last use ranged from 1 to 24 hours prior to data collection (mean = 888 minutes, SD = 755.86). Cannabis vape users primarily described stick or "box mod" rechargeable batteries with disposable cannabis cartridges. Cannabis vape participants reported use of a variety of temperature settings on their devices. Duration since last use ranged from 15 minutes to 10 hours prior to data collection (mean = 164 minutes, SD = 246.26). When combining the two vape groups into the "all vape users" group, duration since last use ranged from 15 minutes to 24 hours prior to data collection (mean = 479.55 minutes, SD = 638.41).

Primary Analysis of Outcome Measures

Means and standard deviations for acoustic analysis, pulmonary function, phonatory and respiratory efficiency, and auditory-perceptual dependent variables by group (nicotine vape user, cannabis vape user, all vape users, and nonsmokers) are presented in Tables 1 through 4, respectively. Medians and semi-interquartile range for the quality of life dependent variable by group are presented in Table 5.

Table 1. Means, Standard Deviations, and Sample Size for Acoustic Analysis Measures by Group

Measure	Nicotine Vape User	Cannabis Vape Users	All Vape Users	Nonsmokers (Control)
F_0 (Hz)				
Mean	163.40	155.67	161.98	185.54
SD	60.50	51.54	51.06	68.22
N	5	5	11	10

	Nicotine Vape User	Cannabis Vape Users	All Vape Users	Nonsmokers (Control)
Jitter %				
Mean	0.394%	0.415%	0.441%	0.324%
SD	0.137%	0.210%	0.199%	0.174%
N	5	5	11	10
Shimmer %				
Mean	2.74%	3.48%	3.66%	3.05%
SD	0.908%	1.48%	2.18%	0.893%
N	5	5	11	10
Shimmer dB				
Mean	0.244	0.308	0.325	0.268
SD	0.082	0.134	0.194	0.079
N	5	5	11	10
HNR (dB)				
Mean	20.63	19.64	19.47	21.38
SD	2.21	4.55	3.91	3.20
N	5	5	11	10
Mean Intensity dB				
Mean	73.02	73.48	72.81	73.50
SD	2.89	4.87	3.87	5.56
N	5	5	11	10

Abbreviations: SD = standard deviation, N = sample size, F_0 = Fundamental Frequency, HNR = Harmonics-to-Noise Ratio

Table 2. Means, Standard Deviations, and Sample Size for Pulmonary Function Measures by Group

Measure	Nicotine Vape User	Cannabis Vape Users	All Vape Users	Nonsmokers (Control)
MIP (cm H_2O)				
Mean	75.20	102.40	93.91	87.09
SD	16.92	22.99	28.25	23.13
N	5	5	11	10
MEP (cm H_2O)				
Mean	108.60	126.20	120.91	107.45
SD	20.95	10.09	20.72	16.93
N	5	5	11	10

Abbreviations: SD = standard deviation, N = sample size, MIP = Maximum Inspiratory Pressure, MEP = Maximum Expiratory Pressure

Table 3. Means, Standard Deviations, and Sample Size for Phonatory and Respiratory Efficiency Measures by Group

Measure	Nicotine Vape User	Cannabis Vape Users	All Vape Users	Nonsmokers (Control)
MPT (s)				
Mean	14.39	22.51	17.87	21.61
SD	6.42	7.82	7.82	4.82
N	5	5	11	10
s/z Ratio				
Mean	1.14	1.11	1.14	0.963
SD	0.380	0.276	0.303	0.263
N	5	5	11	10

Abbreviations: SD = standard deviation, N = sample size, MPT = Maximum Phonation Time

Table 4. Means, Standard Deviations, and Sample Size for Auditory-Perceptual Measure (CAPE-V) by Group

Measure	Nicotine Vape User	Cannabis Vape Users	All Vape Users	Nonsmokers (Control)
Overall Severity				
Mean	3.20	3.00	3.18	1.82
SD	2.95	4.47	3.40	2.96
N	5	5	11	10
Roughness				
Mean	5.00	2.60	3.45	2.64
SD	3.74	4.34	3.98	3.85
N	5	5	11	10
Breathiness				
Mean	0.40	2.00	1.82	1.45
SD	0.894	2.74	2.86	2.58
N	5	5	11	10
Strain				
Mean	2.00	1.00	1.36	0.64
SD	4.47	2.24	3.23	2.11
N	5	5	11	10
Pitch				
Mean	0	0	0	0
SD	0	0	0	0
N	5	5	11	10

Loudness				
Mean	0	0	0.36	0.27
SD	0	0	1.21	0.91
N	5	5	11	10

Abbreviations: SD = standard deviation, N = sample size

Table 5. Median, Semi-Interquartile Range, and Sample Size for Quality of Life Measure (VHI-10) by Group

Measure	Nicotine Vape User	Cannabis Vape Users	All Vape Users	Nonsmokers (Control)
VHI-10 Score				
Median	7	6	6	1
SQR	3	3.5	2	3
N	5	5	11	10

Abbreviations: SQR = semi-interquartile range, N = sample size

Analysis of Group Differences

Research Question 1 aimed to examine whether perceptual and instrumental objective measures of voice and respiratory pressure differ among vape users, conventional cigarette smokers, and non-users. However, since cigarette smokers that fit eligibility criteria were unable to be recruited and accrual to the nicotine and cannabis vape groups was limited, the statistical plan outlined in the methodology was not followed. Instead, two group comparisons for matched groups (i.e., the "all vape users" compared to all sex and age-matched controls, nicotine vape users compared to their sex and age-matched controls, and cannabis vape users compared to their sex and age-matched controls) were all assessed using the Wilcoxon Signed Rank test across all measures.

Table 6 summarizes the inferential statistics for the acoustic analysis, pulmonary function, and phonatory and respiratory efficiency measures for the "all vape users" group and the control group. Table 7 includes the inferential statistics for the auditory-perceptual and quality of life measures. When comparing all vape

users to their sex and age-matched controls, no significant differences were found

with respect to acoustic analysis, pulmonary function, phonatory and respiratory

efficiency, and auditory-perceptual measures. There was, however, a significant

difference when comparing the quality of life measure of the VHI-10 scores, with

the "all vape users" group scoring significantly higher than the control group (p =

0.028). Median VHI-10 scores for the "all vape users" group compared to the non-

user control group can be seen in Figure 4.

Table 6. Inferential Statistics for Acoustic Analysis, Pulmonary Function, and Phonatory and
Respiratory Efficiency Measures of All Vape Users Group compared to Control Group

Measure		F_0 (Hz)	Jitter %	Shimmer %	Shimmer dB	HNR (dB)
	Z	- 1.60	- 1.423	- 0.978	- 0.978	- 1.334
Sig. (2-tailed)		0.110	0.155	0.328	0.328	0.182
Measure		Mean Intensity dB	MIP (cm H_2O)	MEP (cm H_2O)	MPT (s)	s/z Ratio
	Z	- 0.711	- 0.624	- 1.292	- 1.156	- 1.689
Sig. (2-tailed)		0.477	0.533	0.196	0.248	0.091

Abbreviations: F_0 = Fundamental Frequency, HNR = Harmonics-to-Noise Ratio, MIP = Maximum
Inspiratory Pressure, MEP = Maximum Expiratory Pressure, MPT = Maximum Phonation Time

Table 7. Inferential Statistics for Auditory-Perceptual (CAPE-V) and Quality of Life Measures of All
Vape Users Group compared to Control Group

Measure	Overall	Roughness	Breathiness	Strain	Pitch	Loudness	VHI-10

	Z	- 1.355	- 1.063	- 0.677	- 0.535	0.000	- 0.447	-2.199*
Sig. (2tailed)		0.176	0.288	0.498	0.593	1.000	0.655	0.028

* Statistically significant difference, $p < 0.05$

Abbreviation: VHI-10 = Voice Handicap Index-10

Figure 4. Median Voice Handicap Index-10 Scores for All Vape Users and Controls

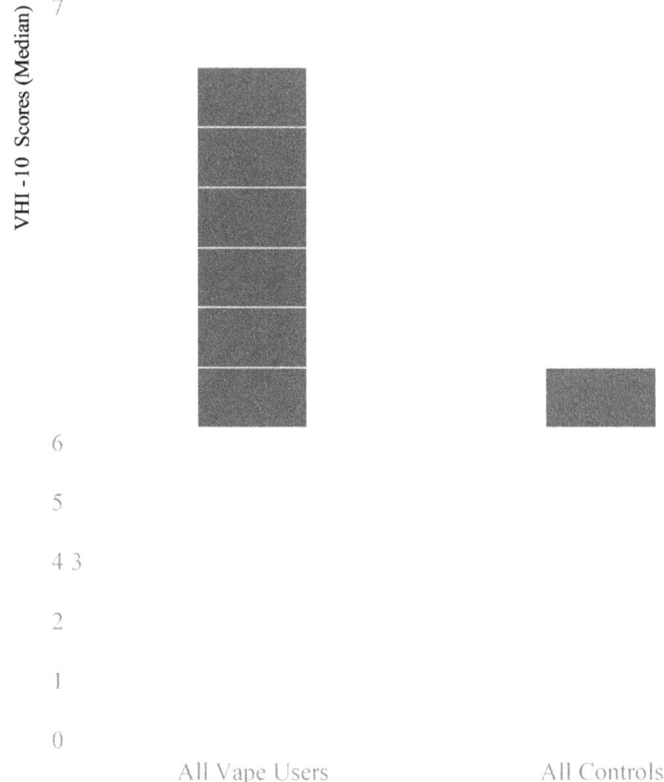

Inferential statistics for the acoustic analysis, pulmonary function, and phonatory and respiratory efficiency measures for the nicotine vape users in comparison to their controls are presented in Table 8. Inferential statistics for the auditory-perceptual and quality of life measures for this comparison can be seen in Table 9. No significant differences were observed across all measures between the nicotine vape group and their matched controls.

Table 8. Inferential Statistics for Acoustic Analysis, Pulmonary Function, and Phonatory and
Respiratory Efficiency Measures of Nicotine Vape Users Group compared to their Controls

Measure	F_0 (Hz)	Jitter %	Shimmer %	Shimmer dB	HNR (dB)
Z	- 0.135	- 0.135	- 0.135	- 0.135	- 0.405
Sig. (2-tailed)	0.893	0.893	0.893	0.893	0.686
Measure	Mean Intensity dB	MIP (cm H_2O)	MEP (cm H_2O)	MPT (s)	s/z Ratio
Z Sig. (2-tailed)	- 0.135	- 0.135	- 0.135	- 1.753	- 1.753
	0.893	0.892	0.892	0.080	0.080

Abbreviations: F_0 = Fundamental Frequency, HNR = Harmonics-to-Noise Ratio, MIP = Maximum Inspiratory Pressure, MEP = Maximum Expiratory Pressure, MPT = Maximum Phonation Time

Table 9. Inferential Statistics for Auditory-Perceptual (CAPE-V) and Quality of Life Measures of
Nicotine Vape Users Group compared to their Controls

Measure	Overall	Roughness	Breathiness	Strain	Pitch	Loudness	VHI-10
Z Sig. (2-tailed)	- 1.633	- 1.890	- 1.342	- 1.000	0.000	- 1.000	- 1.461
	0.102	0.059	0.180	0.317	1.000	0.317	0.144

Abbreviation: VHI-10 = Voice Handicap Index-10

Table 10 shows the inferential statistics for the acoustic analysis, pulmonary function, and phonatory and respiratory efficiency measures for the cannabis vape users compared to their controls. Table 11 contains the inferential

statistics for the auditory-perceptual and quality of life measures. For the cannabis

vape users and their non-smoking control matches, no significant differences were

found across all measures between the two groups.

Table 10. Inferential Statistics for Acoustic Analysis, Pulmonary Function, and
Phonatory and

Respiratory Efficiency Measures of Cannabis Vape Users Group compared to their
Controls

Measure	F_0 (Hz)	Jitter %	Shimmer %	Shimmer dB	HNR (dB)
Z	- 1.753	- 1.483	- 0.674	- 0.674	- 0.944
Sig. (2-tailed)	0.080	0.138	0.500	0.500	0.345
	Mean Intensity dB	MIP (cm H_2O)	MEP (cm H_2O)	MPT (s)	s/z Ratio
Z Sig. (2-tailed)	- 0.674	- 0.135	- 1.21	- 0.405	- 0.405
	0.500	0.893	0.225	0.686	0.686

Abbreviations: F_0 = Fundamental Frequency, HNR = Harmonics-to-Noise Ratio, MIP = Maximum Inspiratory
Pressure, MEP = Maximum Expiratory Pressure, MPT = Maximum Phonation Time

Table 11. Inferential Statistics for Auditory-Perceptual (CAPE-V) and Quality of Life
Measures of

Cannabis Vape Users Group compared to their Controls

Measure	Overall	Roughness	Breathiness	Strain	Pitch	Loudness	VHI-10
Z	- 0.535	0.000	- 1.414	- 0.447	0.000	0.000	- 1.461
Sig. (2-tailed)	0.593	1.000	0.157	0.655	1.000	1.000	0.144

Abbreviation: VHI-10 = Voice Handicap Index-10

In order to determine whether the substance type (nicotine vs cannabis)

inhaled via a vape impacts the perceptual and instrumental objective measures of

vocal function and respiratory pressure, the Mann-Whitney U test was performed to

determine differences across all measures between the nicotine vape user and

cannabis vape user groups. Inferential statistics for the acoustic analysis, pulmonary function, and phonatory and respiratory efficiency measures for the nicotine vape

users compared to the cannabis vape users are summarized in Table 12. Inferential

statistics for the auditory-perceptual and quality of life measures for this

comparison are included in Table 13. No significant differences were detected

between the nicotine and cannabis vape users groups across all measures.

Table 12. Inferential Statistics for Acoustic Analysis, Pulmonary Function, and Phonatory and
Respiratory Efficiency Measures of Nicotine Vape Users Group compared to Cannabis Vape Users Group

Measure		F_0 (Hz)	Jitter %	Shimmer %	Shimmer dB	HNR (dB)
	U	12.000	12.000	9.000	9.000	8.000
Sig. (2-tailed)		0.917	0.917	0.465	0.465	0.347
		Mean Intensity dB	MIP (cm H_2O)	MEP (cm H_2O)	MPT (s)	s/z Ratio
	U	12.000	4.000	5.000	4.000	12.000
Sig. (2-tailed)		0.917	0.073	0.117	0.076	0.917

Abbreviations: F_0 = Fundamental Frequency, HNR = Harmonics-to-Noise Ratio, MIP = Maximum Inspiratory
Pressure, MEP = Maximum Expiratory Pressure, MPT = Maximum Phonation Time

Table 13. Inferential Statistics for Auditory-Perceptual (CAPE-V) and Quality of Life Measures of
Nicotine Vape Users Group compared to Cannabis Vape Users Group

Measure		Overall	Roughness	Breathiness	Strain	Pitch	Loudness	VHI-10
	U	10.500	7.000	9.000	12.000	12.500	12.500	11.500
Sig. (2-tailed)		0.665	0.240	0.366	0.881	1.000	1.000	0.834

Abbreviation: VHI-10 = Voice Handicap Index-10

Because cigarette smokers that fit eligibility criteria for this study could

not be recruited, the impact of delivery method for nicotine products (nicotine vapes

vs conventional cigarettes) on the perceptual and instrumental objective measures

of vocal function and respiratory pressure could not be determined.

Analysis of Relationships Among Measures

Research question 2 was intended to examine possible patterns among the perceptual, objective, and quality of life measures that might distinguish among the subject groups. Because of the small sample size, data were insufficient to support a true multivariate solution; however, the following steps were taken on an exploratory basis.

To answer question 2a, the bivariate intercorrelations among the objective and subjective outcome measures were calculated. Appendix Table A includes the intercorrelations among the objective measures (acoustic analysis, pulmonary function, and phonatory and respiratory efficiency). Statistically significant intercorrelations among these measures include: 1) jitter % with shimmer %, shimmer dB, and HNR, 2) shimmer % with shimmer dB, HNR, MIP, and MEP, 3) shimmer dB with HNR and MEP, 4) HNR with mean intensity dB and MEP, and 5) MIP with

MEP. Appendix Table B includes the intercorrelations among the subjective measures (CAPE-V, VHI-10). Statistically significant intercorrelations among these measures include: 1) the overall severity score with the roughness score on the CAPE-V and 2) the breathiness rating with the loudness rating on the CAPE-V. Appendix Table C includes the intercorrelations among all objective and subjective measures. Statistically significant intercorrelations among all objective and subjective measures include: 1) jitter % with the breathiness and loudness ratings on the CAPE-V, 2) shimmer % with the breathiness and loudness ratings, 3) shimmer dB with the breathiness and loudness ratings, and 4) HNR with the overall severity rating.

Because there were no accruals to the cigarette smoking group, question 2b could not be answered. In order to answer question 2c, first, all outcome measures between the nicotine vape and cannabis vape groups that had a level of significance on the Mann-Whitney U test of $p \leq 0.30$ were identified. These were potential candidates for predictor variables in a binomial logistic regression analysis. The candidate predictor variables were MPT, MIP, MEP, and the roughness ratings on the CAPE-V. Refer to Tables 12 and 13 for the levels of significance for these variables.

After candidate predictors were identified, the intercorrelations in Appendix Tables A, B, and C were examined to determine those variables that were least redundant among the candidates. The goal was to select a measure from each of the outcome domains (acoustic analysis, pulmonary function, phonatory and respiratory efficiency, auditory-perceptual, and QoL). The final selection of measures included MIP, MPT, and the roughness rating. MPT was not intercorrelated with any other variable, and it was the only phonatory and respiratory efficiency measure with $p \leq 0.30$. MIP was selected as the representative for pulmonary function since it correlated moderately with MEP ($r = 0.649$), indicating potential redundancy. Lastly, the roughness rating on the CAPE-V was the only candidate subjective measure and therefore was chosen for the regression analysis.

Using the Forward Stepwise method, MPT, MIP, and roughness rating were entered into a binomial logistic regression model to examine the relationship between the predictor variables and group membership in either the nicotine or

cannabis vape groups. Table 14 presents the results of the binomial logistic

regression. The regression model with MIP was significant ($X^2 = 4.054$, $df = 1$, $p = 0.044$). No other predictors were maintained in the model. MIP correctly classified

70.0% of cases. The odds of being classified in the cannabis vape group increase by

1.40% ($Exp[B*5 \text{ cmH}_2 0]$) for each 5 cmH$_2$O increase in MIP.

Table 14. Binomial Logistic Regression for Maximum Inspiratory Pressure

	B	S.E.	Wald	df	Sig.	Exp(B)
Step 1 MIP	0.068	0.041	2.759	1	0.097	1.070
Constant	- 6.022	3.698	2.6529	1	0.103	0.002

Abbreviations: MIP = Maximum Inspiratory Pressure, S.E. = Standard Error, df = Degrees of Freedom

Secondary Analysis of Outcome Measures

Before data collection, all vape participants were asked user history

questions including when they last used their product, how many years they have

used their product, and approximately how many puffs they take per day.

Correlation analysis was completed to assess the relationship among all objective

and subjective measures with the user history data for all vape users. Tables 15 and

16 present these correlations. Statistically significant findings include time since

last puff with F_0 ($p = 0.031$) and the roughness rating on the CAPE-V ($p = 0.025$),

and puffs per day with time since last puff ($p - 0.004$).

Table 15. Correlations for Objective Measures with User History

Measures	Time since last puff (min)	Years of Vape Use	Puffs per Day
F$_0$ (Hz)			
Pearson's r	- 0.650*	- 0.285	- 0.419
Sig. (2-tailed)	0.031	0.395	0.200
Jitter %			
Pearson's r	0.042	0.137	- 0.019
Sig. (2-tailed)	0.901	0.688	0.957
Shimmer %			
Pearson's r	- 0.252	0.068	- 0.273
Sig. (2-tailed)	0.455	0.842	0.416
Shimmer dB			
Pearson's r	- 0.264	0.051	- 0.282
Sig. (2-tailed)	0.433	0.882	0.400
HNR (dB)			
Pearson's r	0.107	- 0.221	0.160
Sig. (2-tailed)	0.754	0.513	0.638

Mean Intensity dB			
Pearson's r	0.059	- 0.017	0.303
Sig. (2-tailed)	0.862	0.960	0.365
MIP (cm H$_2$O)			
Pearson's r	- 0.176	0.302	- 0.084
Sig. (2-tailed)	0.605	0.366	0.806
MEP (cm H$_2$O)			
Pearson's r	- 0.141	0.178	- 0.206
Sig. (2-tailed)	0.680	0.601	0.543
MPT (s)			
Pearson's r	0.170	- 0.341	- 0.249
Sig. (2-tailed)	0.618	0.304	0.460
s/z Ratio			
Pearson's r	- 0.320	0.389	- 0.225
Sig. (2-tailed)	0.337	0.237	0.507

* Statistically significant difference, $p < 0.05$

a. Cannot be computed because at least one of the variables is constant.

Abbreviations: F_0 = Fundamental Frequency, HNR = Harmonics-to-Noise Ratio, MIP = Maximum Inspiratory Pressure, MEP = Maximum Expiratory Pressure, MPT = Maximum Phonation Time

Table 16. Correlations for Subjective Measures with User History

Measures	Time since last puff (min)	Years of Vape Use	Puffs per Day
Overall Score (CAPE-V)			
Pearson's r	0.270	- 0.334	-0.112
Sig. (2-tailed)	0.422	0.315	0.743
Roughness (CAPE-V)			
Pearson's r	0.665*	- 0.236	0.219
Sig. (2-tailed)	0.025	0.485	0.517

Breathiness (CAPE-V)			
Pearson's r	- 0.481	0.350	- 0.271
Sig. (2-tailed)	0.134	0.291	0.419
Strain (CAPE-V)			
Pearson's r	0.371	- 0.046	0.301
Sig. (2-tailed)	0.261	0.892	0.368
Pitch (CAPE-V)			
Pearson's r			
Sig. (2-tailed)	a	a	a
Loudness (CAPE-V)			
Pearson's r	- 0.241	0.055	- 0.191
Sig. (2-tailed)	0.475	0.873	0.573
VHI-10 Scores			
Spearman Correlation	0.023	0.089	0.075
Sig. (2-tailed)	0.946	0.795	0.826
Time since last puff (min)			
Pearson's r	—	0.034	0.790*
Sig. (2-tailed)		0.922	0.004
Years of Vape Use			
Pearson's r	—	—	0.336
Sig. (2-tailed)			0.312

* Statistically significant difference, $p < 0.05$

a. Cannot be computed because at least one of the variables is constant.

Because of the small sample size in this study, there was limited power to

detect significant differences between some groups on various dependent variables.

For outcomes measures that had a significance level of $p \leq 0.30$ but greater than $p =$

0.05 for either the "all vape users" group versus their matched controls and the

comparison of nicotine versus cannabis vape users, effect size was calculated using

G*Power ver.3.1.9.6. For each measure, the effect size was used to determine the sample size that would be needed to detect group significance at $p \leq 0.05$. Table 17 summarizes the effect size and estimated number of pairs needed to determine significance between the "all vape users" group and their matched controls, and Table 18 includes the number of subjects per group needed to achieve significance between nicotine vape users and cannabis vape users.

In order to detect significant differences between the "all vape users" group and their matched controls, required sample sizes range from 30 pairs for s/z ratio to 255 pairs for roughness. More power was detected between the nicotine and cannabis vape groups, with required sample sizes ranging from 13 per group for MIP to 63 per group for roughness.

Table 17. Power calculations for All Vape Users versus Control Group based upon effect size for all outcome measures with a significant level of $p \leq 0.30$

Measure	Significance Level	Effect Size	Estimated Number of Pairs Needed
F_0	0.110	0.38	75
Jitter %	0.155	0.30	119
HNR (dB)	0.182	0.53	40
MPT (s)	0.248	0.55	38
s/z Ratio	0.091	0.62	30
Overall Severity (CAPE-V)	0.176	0.42	62
Roughness (CAPE-V)	0.288	0.21	255

Abbreviations: HNR = Harmonics-to-Noise Ratio, MPT = Maximum Phonation Time

Table 18. Power calculations for Nicotine Vape versus Cannabis vape group based upon effect size for all outcome measures with a significance level of $p \leq 0.30$

Measure	Significance Level	Effect Size	Estimated Number of Subjects Needed per Group
MIP (cm H_2O)	0.073	1.35	13
MEP (cm H_2O)	0.117	0.92	27
MPT (s)	0.076	1.14	18
Roughness (CAPE-V)	0.240	0.59	63

Abbreviations: HNR = Harmonics-to-Noise Ratio, MEP = Maximum Expiratory Pressure, MPT = Maximum Phonation Time

DISCUSSION

The present study aimed to examine the possible effects of vape products on perceptual and instrumental objective measures of voice in a sex and age-matched sample. As the number of substances available to vape on the market have grown to include more than solely nicotine products, this study likewise endeavored to compare potential differences between the two most commonly vaped substances—nicotine versus cannabis. No study to date has investigated this difference in a controlled laboratory setting. To contribute to the literature targeting the question of how vaping impacts the voice compared to traditional cigarette smoking, this study also attempted to include a cigarette smoking group for this juxtaposition. Nevertheless, cigarette smoking subjects that fit eligibility criteria could not be recruited. This challenge resulted in a study comparing a combined nicotine vape users and cannabis vape users group (the "all vape users" group) to a sex and age-matched control group of non-smokers, along with comparisons of each substance type separately to their controls, and a comparison of nicotine versus cannabis vape users to examine the difference in substance type vaped.

One statistically significant finding between groups was observed in this study when considering the possible impact of vaping on voice quality. When comparing the combined "all vape users" group to the sex and age-matched control group of nonsmokers, the vape users selfrated significantly higher (worse) scores on the Voice Handicap Index-10 compared to their controls, where higher scores correlate with increasingly negative quality of life due to voice concerns. No other significant differences were observed between nicotine vape users alone and their matched controls, cannabis vape users alone and their matched controls, and when comparing nicotine to cannabis vape users. Through use of a binomial logistic regression analysis, it was determined that MIP was the strongest predictor of group classification.

Interpretation of Results: Research Question 1

Research Question 1 inquired, "Do the perceptual and instrumental objective measures of voice and respiratory pressure differ among vape users, conventional cigarette smokers, and nonusers?" The full extent of this question could not be answered in this study as conventional cigarette smokers that fit eligibility criteria could not be recruited. The primary challenge for accrual of this population included recruitment of cigarette smokers that belonged to the required age range of 18 to 35 years. This chosen age range was intended to reflect the higher percentage of vape use seen among the young adult population as 20% of adults ages 18-29 reported regular or occasional vape use in 2018, which decreased to 8% when shifting the age range to 30 to 64 years (Newport, 2018). Likewise, in order to accurately compare vocal acoustics, it was necessary to limit this age range to ensure subjects could be sex and age-matched within 3 years to avoid age related changes of the larynx that may impact acoustic and perceptual measurements (Ferrand, 2019). The fact that cigarette smokers ages 18 to 35 could not be recruited for the purposes of this study is not surprising given the report from the National Center for Chronic Disease Prevention and Health Promotion Office on Smoking and Health that vaping has surpassed conventional tobacco products as the most frequently used form of tobacco among youth and young adults in the US. Research

Question 1 was therefore adjusted to examine differences solely among vape users and the control group who are non-smokers and non-vape users, and Research Question 1b ("Does the delivery method for nicotine products [nicotine vapes vs conventional cigarettes] impact the perceptual and instrumental objective measures of vocal function and respiratory pressure?) could not be answered. In addition, it was required to allow for less restrictive exclusion criteria for the vape user groups as 3 of the 11 vape users

(27.3%) reported "occasional" dual use of nicotine and cannabis vapes (with only one participant who indicated daily use of both), and 5 of the 11 vape users (45.5%) described "social" use of combustible cannabis. Dual use is a barrier to well-defined participant groups given reports from Buckner et al. (2021) that among young adult undergraduate students that use nicotine vapes, over 50% endorse dual use of cannabis. Without leniency to dual usage of products, recruitment for this study would have been severely limited.

The nicotine vape users and cannabis vape users were combined into an "all vape users" group and compared to their sex and age-matched controls of never-smokers. One statistically significant difference was observed across all objective and subjective measures in this analysis. The Voice Handicap Index-10 (VHI-10) is a 10 question self-rated quality of life assessment subjectively examining individual perceptions of and experiences with their voices (Rosen et al., 2004). A higher score on the VHI-10 is associated with an increased negative quality of life due to voice concerns, with scores above 11 considered as abnormal and linked to possible vocal pathology (Arffa et al., 2012). The "all vape users" group scored significantly higher on the VHI10 compared to their controls, with a median score of 6 for the vape users compared to 1 for the nonsmokers. This statistically significant higher median score suggests the vapers have increased self-perceived negative quality of life as it relates to their voice compared to the nonsmokers, despite both group medians falling within normal limits. Average duration of use among all vapers was 5.27 years, and it is possible that continued vape use may lead to further increased VHI-10 scores given the evidence of increased self-reported negative health-related quality of life with continued traditional cigarette use (Sarna et al., 2008).

Nicotine vape users alone were compared to their sex and age-matched controls. There were no significant differences across all objective and subjective measures. This finding suggests that the delivery method of nicotine via a vape may have less adverse effects on voice quality compared to that of traditional cigarettes, given the significant literature base that defines the negative impact of cigarette smoking on voice quality (Byeon & Cha, 2020). It is worth consideration, though, that the phonatory and respiratory efficiency measures of maximum phonation time (MPT) and s/z ratio along with the perceptual rating of roughness for this comparison are close to significance ($p = 0.080$, $p = 0.080$, and $p = 0.059$, respectively). This brings into question whether continued vape use and increased sample sizes may lead to significant differences in these areas.

Cannabis vape users alone were compared to their sex and age-matched controls. Across all objective and subjective measures, no significant differences were observed. Similar to the results of nicotine vaping, this preliminary finding suggests that the delivery method of cannabis via a vape may have less adverse effects on voice quality compared to combustible cannabis, as the current understanding of combustible cannabis is that its impact on the voice is similar to that of conventional cigarette smoking (Balouch et al., 2022; Meehan-Atrash et al., 2019).

Research Question 1a asks, "Does the substance type (nicotine vs cannabis) inhaled via a vape impact the perceptual and instrumental objective measures of vocal function and respiratory pressure?" When analyzing all measures between the nicotine vape users and cannabis vape users, no statistically significant differences were found. This preliminary finding suggests that inhalation of different substance types via a vape do not impact the voice in different ways. However, when assessing nicotine versus cannabis inhalation in any functional or physiological domain, it is important to recognize the difference in frequency of use among the substances, as nicotine products were used notably more in one day compared to cannabis products. In this study, the nicotine vape users group self-reported an average of 68 puffs per day whereas the cannabis vape users group reported an average of 13.5 puffs per day. It is worth consideration that high frequency users of vape products may be at increased risk of adverse voice and pulmonary effects given the current literature that repeated inhalation of nicotine via a vape leads to reduced pulmonary function (Tsai et al., 2020).

Interpretation of Results: Research Question 2

Research Question 2 asks, "Are there patterns of perceptual, objective, and quality of life measures that distinguish among the subject groups?" As outlined in the results section, there were insufficient data to support a true multivariate solution due to the small sample sizes in this study, thus various steps were taken to answer Research Question 2 on an exploratory basis. Due to no accruals to the cigarette smoking group, Research Question 2b ("What combinations of these measures tend to discriminate between delivery method groups [nicotine vapes vs conventional cigarettes]?") could not be answered.

The intercorrelations among the objective and subjective measures were calculated and a set of statistically significant intercorrelations were identified to answer Research Question 2a, "What are the correlational relationships among the clinician-rated perceptual measures, the instrumental objective measures, and the subject-rated quality of life measures of vocal function?" The primary purpose for investigating the intercorrelations among all measures was to identify redundancy in order to reduce the number of potential predictors for the regression analysis that was completed to answer Research Question 2c. The significant intercorrelations identified follow logical patterns. Many of the acoustic measures are intercorrelated, the pulmonary function measures are intercorrelated, and select auditory-perceptual measures are intercorrelated. The acoustic measure of shimmer is also correlated with the pulmonary function measures of MIP and maximum expiratory pressure (MEP). Shimmer is an acoustic perturbation measure that signifies variations in amplitude (dB) of the voice—it is predictable then that shimmer would be correlated with pulmonary function measures, as the primary mechanism for increased loudness is through increased respiratory effort in conjunction with increased tension in the vocal folds (Ferrand, 2002). Likewise for similar reasons, there are logical observed intercorrelations of jitter and shimmer with the auditory-perceptual measures of breathiness and loudness. As shimmer is correlated with pulmonary function measures, a correlation with perceptual vocal qualities that are related to breath support is appropriate. Comparably, as increased jitter is associated with deviant voice characteristics such as roughness and hoarseness, it is reasonable to expect correlations with other perceptual deviant voice characteristics.

A binomial logistic regression analysis was completed to address Research Question 2c, "What combinations of these measures tend to discriminate between substance type (nicotine vs cannabis) inhaled via a vape?" This analysis determined that MIP was the strongest predictor of group classification, as the binomial logistic regression model incorporating MIP correctly classified 70.0% of cases in this study. This finding aligns with the current literature base that reports adverse pulmonary effects seen with vape use (Tsai et al., 2020). It is important to note, however, that this regression analysis is only exploratory, as best practice for multivariate analysis includes at least 10 observations at each dichotomized level per predictor (Agresti, 2012). The nicotine and cannabis vape user groups included only 5 subjects each. It is plausible that with sufficient sample sizes, other variables may have become significant predictors of group membership. This possibility is discussed in the Interpretation of Secondary Analyses section.

Interpretation of Secondary Analyses

As the user history for all vape users varied (i.e., years of vape use, approximate puffs per day, and time since last puff), correlation analysis was completed to assess the possible relationships among these data and all the objective and subjective measures of vocal function. The statistically significant correlations include time since last puff with the acoustic measure of fundamental frequency (F_0) and the subjective roughness rating on the CAPE-V, and puffs per day correlated with time since last puff. The latter is a logical correlation, as an increased number of puffs per day increases the chance that an individual would have used their product close to the time of data collection. The former correlations of time since last puff with F_0 and roughness are worth further consideration. F_0 is the acoustic correlate of what is perceived as pitch in the voice. These correlations suggest that vapers are more likely to demonstrate changes in F_0 and be perceived by others as having a rougher voice closer to the time of last vape use. Although the correlation between F_0 and roughness was not significant, it did demonstrate a moderate correlation of $r = -0.458$ (Appendix Table C). In an attempt to reduce extraneous variables, all vape users were asked to refrain from using their products for at least 30 minutes prior to the data collection session. One participant reported use 25 minutes prior, and two reported use 15 minutes prior. Of these three participants, one female vape user that reported use 15 minutes prior to data collection demonstrated a lower average F_0 (186.39 Hz) compared to all female group averages (see Appendix Table E) and this average likewise fell outside of the normative range for female F_0 of 209-256.82 Hz (Kent et al., 2023). It is also worth noting that this subject was the only individual that reported daily use of both nicotine and cannabis vapes, however, the product used prior to data collection was not specified. These findings echo what is cited as one of the most significant impacts of traditional smoking on the voice—the lowering of F_0 (Byeon & Cha, 2020).

Means and standard deviations for all sex-dependent objective measures are broken down by group and sex in Appendix Tables D and E. Normative values for vocal acoustics, pulmonary function, and phonatory and respiratory efficiency measures are reported separately by sex due to anatomical differences in males and females that impact these values. Many of the group averages values fell within normal limits, however, there are notable deviations. In continuing the discussion of lowering F_0, the female cannabis vape users group demonstrated a lower average F_0 outside of normal limits despite the combined male and female group averages demonstrating no significant difference. Meehan-Atrash et al. (2019) and Valentino & McKinnon (2019) report many similarities between traditional cigarette smoking and traditional cannabis smoking in its impact on voice quality including observed differences in vocal pitch. This finding suggests that vaping cannabis may have similar adverse effects. In addition, both male and female nicotine vape users demonstrated lower group averages that fell outside of normal limits in the phonatory and respiratory efficiency measure of maximum phonation time (MPT). This measure is defined as the longest duration in which an individual can sustain consistent vowel production. This finding for nicotine vape users parallels the other most significant impact of traditional smoking on the voice—reduction of MPT (Byeon & Cha, 2020).

MIP is the last notable measure that fell outside of normal limits for several groups including all male subject groups as well as female nicotine vape users and female control subjects. It is important to recognize, however, that whether these values fall within or outside of normal limits is dependent on the study in which the normative values are obtained. Sclauser et al. (2014) completed a systematic review of 22 studies to provide normative MIP ranges for adults in age groups ranging from 18-29 to 70-83. If using the normative values provided by this systematic review, all male subject groups along with female nicotine vape users and the female control group MIP averages fall below normal limits. Conversely, Gil Obando et al. (2012) completed an observational descriptive study assessing both MIP and MEP in healthy adults in Manizales, Colombia. This study provided the normative data for MEP as a systematic review of normative values for this measure in healthy adults similar to Sclauser et al. (2014) could not be found. When using the normative values provided by Gil Obando et al. (2012), all groups fall within normal limits with respect to MIP. Nevertheless, it is important to consider these differences as MIP was the strongest predictor of group classification along with the fact that the current literature primarily highlights adverse cardiopulmonary effects seen with vape use (Tsai et al., 2020).

There was limited power to detect significant differences between some groups on various dependent variables due to the small sample size in this study. Effect sizes were calculated and used to determine the sample size that would be needed to detect group significance for the "all vape users" group versus their matched controls as well as the nicotine versus cannabis vape users group (Tables 17 and 18). An effect size □ 0.8 is considered to be a large effect (Cohen, 1988), and three measures demonstrate an effect size of this magnitude in the nicotine versus cannabis vape comparison. No effect sizes for "all vape users" versus their matched controls fall within this range, however, three measures fall within the moderate effect size range of $0.5 - 0.8$ for this comparison. This suggests that although no significant differences were observed in this study when contrasting nicotine versus cannabis vape users, if sample sizes increase, it is highly likely that significant differences will be found in at least one measure of the two domains of pulmonary function and phonatory and respiratory efficiency measures. The possibility of significant differences between these two substances in the context of vaping and its impact on voice quality is intriguing and worth further investigation considering the current understanding that traditional cigarette and cannabis smoking are relatively similar in terms of their adverse effects on voice quality (Meehan-Atrash et al., 2019). It is possible, however, that these differences may be due to patterns of use between substances (i.e., increased puffs per day seen with nicotine use compared to cannabis) rather than the difference in substance type itself. Given sufficient sample size, puffs per day could be included as a covariate in future statistical analyses.

Relationship of Results to Previous Research

The present study reports one statistically significant finding that has not

yet been observed in the few previous studies examining vapes and their impact on

voice quality. The cross-sectional study completed by Tuhanioğlu et al. (2019)

included 81 healthy adult men that belonged to nicotine vape user, conventional

cigarette user, and nonsmoker groups. They found significant differences only in

the cigarette smoking group, as this group demonstrated higher (worse) VHI-10

scores, higher (deviant) shimmer dB, and lower harmonics-to-noise ratio (a measure

of the degree of additive noise in voice production, where lower values signify

increased additive noise [Ferrand, 2002]) compared to both the vape users and

nonsmoking control group (Tuhanioğlu et al., 2019). No significant differences

were reported by Tuhanioğlu et al. (2019) between the nicotine vape users and

nonsmoker group. As the present study was unable to include a cigarette smoker

group, the discussion comparing the two studies is limited to their report of no

significant differences between the vape user group and nonsmoker group. The

finding of no significant acoustic differences across all groups in the present study

supports and strengthens this evidence provided by Tuhanioğlu et al. (2019),

especially given the fact that the current study included a sex and age-matched

sample whereas Tuhanioğlu et al. (2019) did not.   This study and Tuhanioğlu et

al. (2019) differ with regard to participant self-reported voice-related quality of life.

The "all vape user" group in the present study self-reported significantly higher

(worse) median VHI-10 scores compared to their nonsmoking controls, despite

these values still falling within normal limits. It is worth consideration, however, that the vape user group in the Tuhanioğlu et al. (2019) study reported only nicotine vape use, whereas the "all vape user" group in the present study included both nicotine and cannabis vape users. This significant difference was not detected when assessing individual substance types and their matched controls alone.

Similar studies conducted by Dingmann (2021) and Sample (2019) compared objective vocal measures across the same three groups as Tuhanioğlu et al. (2019). Dingmann (2021) reported no significant differences in acoustic measures or the Voice Handicap Index (VHI) among 18 total participants (4 male and 2 female nicotine vape users, 3 male cigarette smokers, and 2 male and 7 female nonsmokers, all aged between 18-25 years). Sample (2019) likewise reported no significant differences in acoustic measures among 17 total participants (5 male and 2 female nicotine vape users, 2 male and 2 female cigarette smokers, and 2 male and 4 female nonsmokers, all aged between 18 and 35 years). The findings of the present study support and strengthen the evidence of these two studies as well given no significant acoustic findings with a sex and age-matched sample recorded in a controlled laboratory setting. Not only did Dingmann (2021) not have an equal distribution of sex across groups in order to properly sex and agematch, but the quality of data collection could not be controlled as voice recordings were completed using each participants' personal computers and built-in microphones in the context of an online Zoom meeting. While Sample (2019) controlled the setting for data collection, a small number of participants limited sex and age-matching. Sample (2019) does note that accruals for their study were limited due to a strict adherence to subjects being excluded from the study if they reported occasional cigarette or marijuana use.

In alignment with Tuhanioğlu et al. (2019), Dingmann (2021) reported no significant difference between groups with regard to VHI scores. As previously stated, the present study differs from these previous findings in detecting a significant increase in VHI-10 scores in the "all vape user" group compared to their nonsmoking controls. This is likely due to the inclusion of two substance types (nicotine and cannabis) for the "all vape group" in the present study compared to just nicotine vape products assessed by Dingmann (2021). This significant difference is not detected in the present study when assessing solely the nicotine vape group.

There are no studies to date that have investigated the impact of cannabis vaping on voice quality. Due to its only recent widespread legalization throughout parts of the US, research in this area is limited. Meehan-Atrash et al. (2019) discuss that the effects of combustible cannabis on voice production appear to be similar to that of tobacco smoking, while Balouch et al. (2022) report that marijuana smokers commonly complain of hoarse, breathy, and weak voice qualities. In the present study, no significant differences were found between the cannabis vape user group and their matched controls, despite one member of this group reporting dual use of nicotine vapes, and three members with limited social use of traditional cannabis. These preliminary findings are suggestive of a difference in delivery method (vape versus conventional cannabis) in its impact on voice quality and that vaping cannabis may have less adverse effects on the voice.

Similarly, there are no previous studies that have considered a difference in the effect of two substance types (nicotine versus cannabis) inhaled via a vape on voice quality. With the current understanding that conventional cigarette and cannabis smoking appears to impact voice quality in a similar way (Balouch et al., 2022; Meehan-Atrash et al., 2019), the present study offers the preliminary suggestion that differences in substance type do not impact the voice in different ways. Therefore, this study suggests that vaping—regardless of substance type—may have less adverse effects on voice quality than traditional forms of smoking. However, through the use of calculated effect sizes, it was determined that more significant differences in the domains of pulmonary function and phonatory and respiratory efficiency measures may be found with increased sample sizes. Further research in this area is necessary to fully assess these possible differences.

Limitations of the Study

This study was primarily limited by small sample sizes. It is shown through the calculated effect sizes the possibility for significant differences in the nicotine versus cannabis vape comparison if group sizes were increased to as few as 13 subjects per group. Similarly, this study was limited by no accruals to the cigarette smoker group within the required age range that would have allowed for an answer to Research Questions 1b and 2c. Because of this, implications of vape use with regard to vocal health in direct comparison to traditional cigarette smoking cannot be discussed.

Dual usage of nicotine vapes with cannabis vapes and traditional cannabis among participants is another limitation to this study as this did not allow for clearly defined groups. This limitation highlights the findings of Buckner et al. (2021) that dual use of nicotine vapes and cannabis is common among young adults. Well defined groups are also limited by a number of factors the researcher needs to consider such as different temperature settings, dry herb versus liquid cannabis vapes, and variable nicotine content in the e-liquids. A further and final limitation to this study is likewise due to participant vape habits. Three participants did not adhere to the request to refrain from product use for at least 30 minutes prior to data collection. As analysis revealed that time since last puff is correlated with differences in F_0 and perceptual ratings of roughness, this added an extraneous variable that was intended to be controlled. However, of the three vape users that used their products within 30 minutes of data collection, only one participant demonstrated deviant values across mean F_0, shimmer %, shimmer dB, HNR, and MPT. This participant was likewise a dual user of both nicotine and cannabis vape products and was placed solely in the "all vape users" group.

Implications of the Study

The findings of this study imply that vape users (including both nicotine and cannabis users) may have increased negative feelings associated with their voice and its impact on their lives compared to that of nonsmokers. Nevertheless, these self-imposed subjective accounts are not supported by any significantly deviant objective acoustic, pulmonary, phonatory and respiratory efficiency, or subjective clinician-rated measures of voice quality seen with vape use. This finding implies that vaping may have fewer adverse effects on voice quality compared to traditional forms of smoking. However, correlation analysis of all measures with user history in this study suggests that vape users may be more likely to demonstrate changes in F_0 and have an increased chance of being perceived as having a rougher voice closer to the time of last use. Given these findings, it is possible that individuals seeking voice therapy who continue to use vape products may maintain lower self-reported voice-related quality of life and exhibit perceptual roughness despite therapeutic interventions.

This is the first study to report on cannabis vaping in comparison to matched controls with respect to voice quality. Considering the accounts in the current literature that traditional cannabis and cigarette smoking appear to be similar in their adverse effects on voice quality, along with the recent in vitro studies examining the damage caused by cigarette smoke extract and e-cigarette extract on vocal fold mucosa (Lungova et al., 2022; Martinez et al., 2023), it is intriguing that no statistically significant differences between the cannabis vape group and their matched controls was observed. These preliminary findings suggest that the effects of cannabis vaping on voice quality may be different compared to that of combustible cannabis. This implication certainly warrants further research.

Lastly, the comparison of substance types vaped (nicotine versus cannabis) reveals that substance type may not impact voice quality in different ways, suggesting that vaping as a whole may have fewer adverse effects on voice quality than combustible forms of smoking. Calculated effect sizes, however, do suggest the chance of observable differences with increasing sample size. These findings—although preliminary—can guide healthcare professionals to educate their vape user patients that despite popular belief, the current literature base shows vape use can have an impact on respiratory function, although it may have less harmful effects on voice quality than traditional smoking. This will allow patients the ability to make an informed decision regarding their smoking habits.

Implications for Future Research

The findings of the present study highlight the need for further research in the area of vaping and its impact on voice quality. Further work in this area, especially with regard to examining differences in substance type vaped, is necessary with increased sample sizes in order to accurately determine the distinctions between nicotine and cannabis vaping. Despite the downward trends in traditional cigarette use among young adults and likely barriers to recruitment of sex and age-matched subjects, further research is necessary to fully assess the differences of nicotine vaping and traditional cigarettes with regard to vocal health. A similar comparison of cannabis vaping to traditional combustible cannabis is needed to accurately establish this difference as well. As technological innovations continue, more substances become available on the market to vape, and new methods of nicotine and cannabis consumption rise in popularity, it will be crucial to consider their respective impacts on human physiology. Furthermore, as vape products are relatively new forms of smoking, further research following continuing vape users over time is needed to assess the long term implications of vaping on

voice quality.

SUMMARY AND CONCLUSION

The purpose of this study was to investigate the possible effects of various vape products and substance types (including nicotine and cannabis) on perceptual and instrumental objective measures of voice in a sex and age-matched sample. The results revealed vape users may selfreport lower voice-related quality of life compared to nonsmokers. No significant acoustic, pulmonary, phonatory and respiratory efficiency, and auditory-perceptual measures were identified when comparing vape users to their matched controls regardless of substance type and when assessing possible differences between substance type vaped. The pulmonary function measure of maximum inspiratory pressure was determined to be the strongest predictor of group classification. Calculation of effect sizes reveal that increased sample size may lead to significant differences observed in this comparison of nicotine versus cannabis vaping in the domains of pulmonary function and phonatory and respiratory efficiency measures. The results of this study direct future research to continue exploring the effects of vape use along with the difference in substance type vaped on voice quality.

www.ingramcontent.com/pod-product-compliance
Lightning Source LLC
LaVergne TN
LVHW010658200726
843507LV00011B/1925